human rights *first*

Detained and Denied in Afghanistan

How to Make U.S. Detention Comply with the Law

May 2011

About Human Rights First

Human Rights First believes that building respect for human rights and the rule of law will help ensure the dignity to which every individual is entitled and will stem tyranny, extremism, intolerance, and violence.

Human Rights First protects people at risk: refugees who flee persecution, victims of crimes against humanity or other mass human rights violations, victims of discrimination, those whose rights are eroded in the name of national security, and human rights advocates who are targeted for defending the rights of others. These groups are often the first victims of societal instability and breakdown; their treatment is a harbinger of wider-scale repression. Human Rights First works to prevent violations against these groups and to seek justice and accountability for violations against them.

Human Rights First is practical and effective. We advocate for change at the highest levels of national and international policymaking. We seek justice through the courts. We raise awareness and understanding through the media. We build coalitions among those with divergent views. And we mobilize people to act.

Human Rights First is a non-profit, non-partisan international human rights organization based in New York and Washington D.C. To maintain our independence, we accept no government funding.

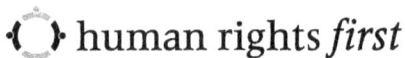

《 》 human rights *first*

New York	**Washington D.C.**
333 Seventh Avenue	100 Maryland Avenue, NE
13th Floor	Suite 500
New York, NY 10001-5108	Washington, DC 20002-5625
Tel.: 212.845.5200	Tel: 202.547.5692
Fax: 212.845.5299	Fax: 202.543.5999

www.humanrightsfirst.org

Acknowledgements

This report was written by Daphne Eviatar, Senior Associate in the Law and Security Program.

It was edited by Gabor Rona, International Legal Director, Dixon Osburn, Director of Law and Security, Tad Stahnke, Director of Policy and Programs, and Elisa Massimino, CEO and President of Human Rights First. Research assistance was provided by Laila Nazaralli, Katie Fourmy, Raha Wala, and Adam Jacobson. Sarah Graham provided production assistance.

Human Rights First would like to thank the many people who helped us in Afghanistan, shared their knowledge and expertise, and spoke with us about their experiences. For their own safety, we will not name those individuals here. We are particularly grateful, however, to the former detainees who travelled from villages and provinces across the country to meet with us in Kabul and share their stories with us. We are also very grateful to the Afghan Human Rights Organization (AHRO), the Afghan Independent Human Rights Commission , (AIHRC), the International Legal Foundation-Afghanistan and the Legal Aid Organization of Afghanistan. Thanks also to the Afghan officials at the Policharky prison who took the time to speak with us and give us a tour of the facility, to the United Nations Assistance Mission in Afghanistan, to the International Crisis Group, and to the Defense Department's Joint Task Force 435 in Afghanistan and Office of Detainee Affairs.

Human Rights First wishes to express its appreciation to our general support and Law & Security donors – both foundations and individuals—who make our research and advocacy possible.

This report is available for free online at www.humanrightsfirst.org

Facts

- Since President Obama took office, the number of prisoners held by the U.S. in Afghanistan has almost tripled—from 600 in 2008 to 1700 in 2011.

- The U.S. Prison at Bagram now holds almost ten times as many detainees as are being held at Guantanamo Bay.

- Prisoners at the U.S.-run Bagram Air Base in Afghanistan now have the right to appear before a board of military officers to plead for their release and challenge the claims that they are "enemy belligerents" fighting U.S. forces.

- Prisoners still do not have the right to see the evidence being used against them, or the right to a lawyer to represent them.

About this Report

This report is based on Human Rights First's observations of hearings provided by the U.S. military for detainees in Afghanistan; interviews with former detainees released from U.S. custody in 2010; interviews with Afghan defense lawyers, prison officials, the Afghan Independent Human Rights Commission and Afghan Human Rights Organization; interviews with international organizations such the International Crisis Group and the United Nations Assistance Mission in Afghanistan; and interviews with and documentation provided by U.S. military and State Department personnel.

At the invitation of the U.S. military, Human Rights First observed three hearings, known as Detainee Review Boards (DRBs), on February 7, 2011and four hearings on September 29, 2010. On February 7, 2011 we also observed an Afghan trial, supported by the U.S. military, taking place at its Parwan Justice Center, part of the U.S.-built Detention Facility in Parwan, located on the Bagram Air Base.

In addition to direct observations of hearings, Human Rights First interviewed 18 former detainees in late 2010 and early 2011, all of whom had been released from U.S. custody within the previous year. Twelve of them had experienced at least one DRB hearing. All interviews were conducted with the assistance of a translator.

Contents

Executive Summary

"They never told me what the evidence was against me. I was asking for it all the time, but no one showed me anything."

–M.G., a former detainee from Khost province

In August 2010, General David Petraeus, Commander of the NATO International Security Assistance Force (ISAF) in Afghanistan, announced a shift in U.S. strategy. The United States "cannot kill or capture our way to victory," he warned. Rather, we must earn the trust of the Afghan people:

> The decisive terrain is the human terrain. The people are the center of gravity. Only by providing them security and earning their trust and confidence can the Afghan government and ISAF prevail.[1]

General Stanley McChrystal, his predecessor, in an August 2009 assessment noted in particular the importance of providing due process to detainees in Afghanistan:

> Detention operations, while critical to successful counterinsurgency operations, also have the potential to become a strategic liability for the U.S. and ISAF. With the drawdown in Iraq and the closing of Guantanamo Bay, the focus on U.S. detention operations will turn to the U.S. Bagram Theater Internment Facility (BTIF). Because of the classification level of the BTIF and the lack of public transparency, the Afghan people see U.S. detention operations as secretive and lacking in due process. It is critical that we continue to develop and build capacity to empower the Afghan government to conduct all detentions operations in this country in accordance with international and national law.[2]

President Obama, for his part, has indicated a strong interest in improving U.S. detention operations and providing detainees due process. As a candidate, he applauded the U.S. Supreme Court's decision granting Guantanamo detainees habeas corpus rights, calling it "a rejection of the Bush administration's attempt to create a legal black hole at Guantanamo" and "an important step toward reestablishing our credibility as a nation committed to the rule of law."[3] Early in his administration, he issued three separate executive orders aimed at improving U.S. detention policy and detainee treatment. And President Obama created a new Joint Task Force to oversee detention operations in Afghanistan and adopted specific new measures to improve detention practices there.

In a July 2010 memorandum, Vice Admiral Robert Harward, the commander of that task force, explained:

> Detention operations are tactical missions with broad-ranging strategic effects. As we separate those who use violence and terror to achieve their aims from the rest of the Afghan population, we must do so in a lawful and humane manner. We have an obligation to treat all Afghan citizens and third-country nationals (TCNs) with dignity and respect. Fulfilling this obligation strengthens our partnership with both the Government of the Islamic Republic of Afghanistan (GIRoA) and the Afghan people. Failure to fulfill this obligation jeopardizes public support for both the Coalition and the GIRoA.[4]

At the very least, these statements and actions imply a commitment by the United States to apply minimum international legal standards of due process to the 1700 or more prisoners now being held without charge or trial at the Bagram U.S. Air Base in Afghanistan.

International law prohibits arbitrary detention. To that end, detention must be based on established law, which must provide the right to challenge the detention, within a short period of time, before an impartial judicial body authorized to order a detainee's release.[5] International legal experts also maintain that detainees should have a right to effective legal assistance, considered "an essential component of the right to liberty of person."[6]

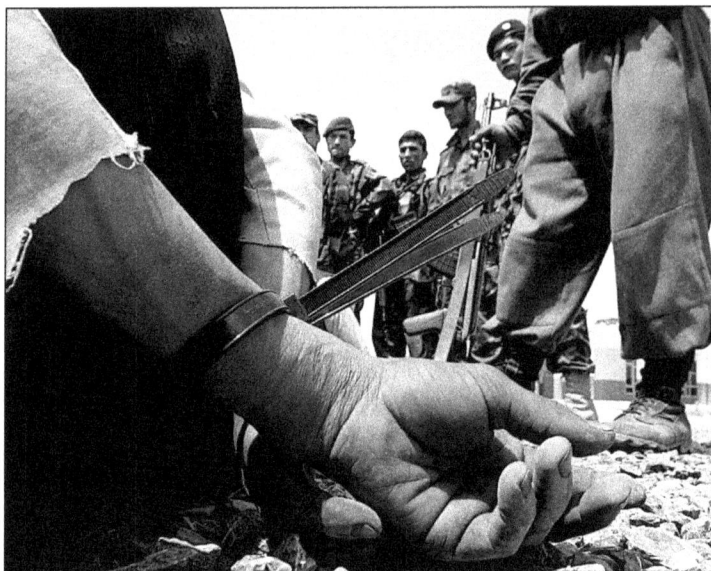

Afghan soldiers look at detained suspected Taliban fighters in Patrol Base Wilson in Zhari district early April 19, 2008.[REUTERS/Goran Tomasevic]

In February 2011, Human Rights First traveled to Afghanistan to determine whether the United States is providing due process to its prisoners there. This trip followed previous ones in recent years that had similarly examined the detention and trials of detainees imprisoned by the U.S. military at Bagram and made recommendations on how to improve the process.[7]

In this latest trip, we found that the U.S. system for determining who is legally detainable has improved since the completely secret process used during the Bush administration. Significantly, the Obama administration now allows detainees to attend at least a portion of a hearing and address a board of U.S. military officers. Each detainee is assigned a "personal representative" to help present his case, and is entitled to a new status hearing every six months. The military has also implemented some of the recommendations that Human Rights First made in its last report, such as allowing human rights organizations to observe detainee hearings; excluding evidence obtained through torture or cruel, inhuman or degrading treatment; and making efforts to improve the

prosecution of national security detainees in Afghan courts.

Nevertheless, based on our observations of proceedings, and interviews with former detainees and U.S. military personnel, we believe that the current system of administrative hearings provided by the U.S. military fails to provide detainees with an adequate opportunity to defend themselves against charges that they are collaborating with insurgents and present a threat to U.S. forces. As such, it not only falls short of the requirements of international law but erodes the critical efforts General Petraeus described as necessary to build trust and confidence among the Afghan people.[8]

Former detainees we interviewed repeatedly emphasized that they believed they were wrongly imprisoned based on false information provided to U.S. forces by personal, family or tribal enemies, a view that they took back to their villages after their eventual release. Afghan lawyers and human rights workers confirmed that this is a big problem in Afghanistan, as have recent news reports.[9] Former detainees said that in the view of their families and communities, the United States is arbitrarily detaining people based on false intelligence. The result, they said, is an increasingly negative perception of U.S. forces.

Moreover, as Major General Douglas Stone warned after investigating U.S. detention practices in Afghanistan in August 2009 for the U.S. Central Command, detaining moderate Afghans unnecessarily risks transforming them into radicals.[10] General Stone, a U.S. Marine Corps reservist, reformed detainee operations in Iraq in 2007 and 2008. His 700-page report on U.S. detention in Afghanistan has never been publicly released.

The United States claims the right to detain insurgents who "were part of, or substantially supported Taliban or al-Qaeda forces or associated forces that are engaged in hostilities against the United States or its coalition partners." In the hearings Human Rights First observed, however, little to no evidence was presented, at least publicly, to support the conclusion that the detainees met this criterion. Not a single witness was called to testify in any of the hearings we observed. In some cases, the evidence against the detainee appeared to be as thin as a mere claim by U.S. soldiers that they found bomb-making materials in a house nearby. No public evidence was presented connecting the individual detainee to that house, or to the materials. In other cases, where the government claimed to have more specific evidence, such as explosive residue found on the detainee's body or clothing, the evidence often raised more questions than it answered, such as whether the residue was found before or after detaining authorities showed the explosive materials to the detainee, and whether he handled them at that time. Yet those questions were never asked.

In large part, that is because the detainees are not represented by legal counsel in these proceedings, known as Detainee Review Boards. The detainees' "personal representatives" are uniformed U.S. soldiers with no legal background or training in the culture or language of the detainees they represent. Moreover, with only 15 such representatives assigned to Bagram at the time of this report, each representative is responsible for the defense of more than 100 detainees. The result, in the cases we

observed, is that these representatives appeared to do little or nothing on behalf of the detainee. Although each is required to attend a 35-hour training course, none seemed to have independently investigated the case, collected evidence on the detainee's behalf, demanded that the government produce evidence, or asked even the most obvious questions challenging the evidence that the government presented.

It is possible that some of these questions were asked in a classified session, which neither the detainee nor Human Rights First was allowed to observe. But that in itself raises serious due process concerns. Even assuming that the government had strong classified evidence in each case to support continued detention of the detainee, the mere reliance on classified evidence detracts from the confidence in the process that the detainee being evaluated—and the people of Afghanistan—are entitled to have.

Moreover, while most forensic evidence, which is more likely to be reliable, is not classified, evidence provided by informants, which is far more difficult to verify, is classified. These informants are never questioned or cross-examined in court, so their veracity is never tested. It is also impossible to know if the classified evidence includes statements elicited from the detainee or from witnesses by coercion, torture, or cruel, inhuman or degrading treatment, despite the military's rule excluding tortured evidence. Such evidentiary rules can only be enforced if the evidence can be tested in a truly adversarial system.

Finally, Human Rights First learned in Afghanistan that even some prisoners who have been recommended for release by the review board of soldiers conducting these hearings remain imprisoned by U.S. authorities. This problem is particularly prevalent for the approximately 41 non-Afghans incarcerated at Bagram. Of these, we believe that more than a dozen have been recommended for transfer or release (the U.S. government will not provide the precise number) yet remain at the U.S. prison. Another unspecified number of Afghans are in the same situation. Despite their responsibility to review all of the evidence, the Detainee Review Boards do not have final authority to order a prisoners release, even if the board determines that the individual does not pose a threat to U.S. forces. This violates international human rights law: the continued incarceration of these individuals is a classic case of arbitrary detention.

The U.S. military now imprisons about ten times as many detainees in Afghanistan as it does at the military prison at Guantanamo Bay. The population of detainees at Bagram has almost tripled since 2008, reaching around 1700 detainees in March.[11] More than 1300 suspects were arrested and imprisoned in 2010 alone, as compared to about 500 arrests in 2009.

Bagram detainees are afforded far fewer rights than are those at Guantanamo. At Guantanamo, detainees have the right to challenge their detention in a U.S. court and to representation by a lawyer. At Bagram, detainees are given only rudimentary hearings. These hearings provide even fewer rights than did the Guantanamo Combatant Status Review Tribunals (CSRT) that the U.S. Supreme Court in 2008 declared inadequate to meet U.S. constitutional obligations.[12]

The result is that some detainees at Bagram have been imprisoned for eight years or more without charge or trial, based largely on evidence they have never seen and with no meaningful opportunity to defend themselves.

Beginning this year, the United States plans to transition at least some of its detention authority to the Government of Afghanistan, and to help the Afghan government improve its detention system and the level of justice it provides to national security detainees. We welcome this development, and appreciated that the U.S. military invited us to observe an Afghan trial held at the Bagram Air Base with the assistance of the U.S. government.

However, our observations at this Afghan trial, as well our conversations with Afghan lawyers and former detainees, reveal that the Afghan justice system is nowhere near providing a minimum level of due process in national security cases. Although detainees are represented by Afghan lawyers in these new Afghan trials held at Bagram, attorneys on both sides still produce little or no relevant evidence. And the judges may rely on secret evidence provided by the Afghan intelligence agency, the National Security Directorate (NDS). The assumption in the case we observed was that all NDS evidence, even if based on unnamed informants, is reliable. As the prosecutor in one case told the court, explaining why the judges should convict a man of membership with the Taliban: "NDS gave us this information. Why would they provide us with wrong information? They have no reason to."[13] The man was convicted, apparently based upon this secret information.

Significantly, the United States has made clear that it intends to retain its detention authority for the indefinite future, even as it continues to transfer some prisoners to Afghan custody. The U.S. military therefore must provide its prisoners a meaningful opportunity to challenge their detention, notwithstanding Afghanistan's future responsibility for this task. Indeed, doing so can help prepare for what will ultimately be a more successful transition to Afghan control of detention operations. Working together with Afghans now to improve the process in both U.S. and Afghan-led review proceedings will contribute to the development of a stable Afghanistan that abides by the rule of law and can resist a takeover by the Taliban or other insurgent forces.

Other democracies that face grave security threats from terrorism, such as Israel, provide independent judicial review, a right to counsel, and appeals to suspected terrorists, and view these as required by international humanitarian law.[14] We see no reason why the United States, which prides itself on respect for the rule of law and human rights, cannot meet the same standards.[15]

Background

"They never told me why they thought I was working with the Taliban. I asked many times if they had any evidence, they never showed me any."

–Tawab, a farmer from Kunar province (arrested in Jalalabad)

Operation Enduring Freedom

The United States, along with NATO allies and the Afghan government, is engaged in an armed conflict with the Taliban and related insurgent groups in Afghanistan.

The U.S.-led Operation Enduring Freedom (OEF) began on October 7, 2001, four weeks after the September 11 attacks on the United States. OEF's counterterrorism mission has been to capture or kill "high-value" Taliban and al Qaeda members, to destroy the safe havens from which al Qaeda planned and directed the September 11 attacks, and to eliminate any future safe havens in Afghanistan.

Since July 2010, U.S. forces Afghanistan (USFOR-A)—which operate under both OEF and NATO/International Security Assistance Force (ISAF) mandates—are under the command of U.S. Army General David Petraeus. U.S. Central Command (CENTCOM), not ISAF, oversees OEF counterterrorism and detainee operations in Afghanistan. The OEF and NATO missions remain separate.

U.S. military forces in Afghanistan operate under a public 2002 diplomatic note that authorizes "cooperative efforts in response to terrorism, humanitarian, and civic assistance, military training and exercises, and other activities."[16]

The diplomatic note does not explicitly mention detention.

The U.S. occupies the Bagram Air Base in Afghanistan pursuant to the "Accommodation Consignment Agreement for Lands and Facilities in Bagram Airfield," which allows the United States and coalition forces "exclusive, peaceable, undisturbed and uninterrupted possession" of Bagram, without charge, for military purposes.[17]

Since March 2009, the Obama administration has claimed the authority to detain "unprivileged enemy belligerents" (formerly known as "unlawful enemy combatants") who meet the following criteria:

> Persons who planned, authorized, committed or aided the terrorist attacks that occurred on September 11, 2001, and persons who harbored those responsible for those attacks;

> Persons who were part of, or substantially supported, Taliban or al Qaeda forces or associated forces that are engaged in hostilities against the United States or its coalition partners, including any person who has committed a belligerent act, or has directly supported hostilities, in aid of such enemy armed forces.[18]

The only difference between this definition and that of "unlawful enemy combatants" used by the Bush administration is the addition of the word "substantially."

Graph showing number of detainees at Bagram, 2004-2011

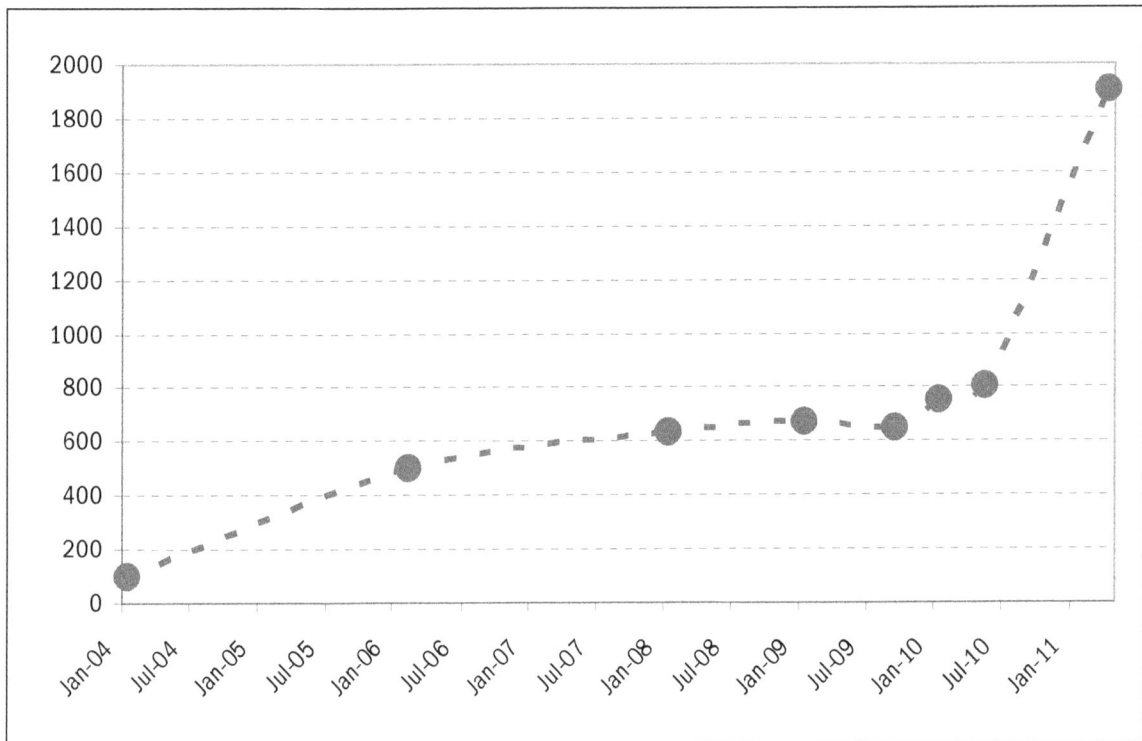

Relevant International Law: The Rights of Detainees in a Non-International Armed Conflict

The United States conflict in Afghanistan is a "non-international armed conflict" in the parlance of International Humanitarian Law. That is because the United States is currently engaged in a war with insurgent groups in Afghanistan rather than with the country's government. (The war was initially an international armed conflict with the Taliban government of Afghanistan.) The cornerstone of International Humanitarian Law, also known as the Laws of Armed Conflict, is the Geneva Conventions. Under the Geneva Conventions, detention of combatants in international armed conflicts is permissible to prevent further participation in hostilities. It is permissible to detain civilians "only if the security of the

Detaining Power makes it absolutely necessary."[19] Although the Geneva Conventions address treatment and trials of detainees in non-international armed conflict, the Conventions do not explicitly authorize detention for such conflicts, as they do for wars between States. The drafters expected that the power to detain in such conflicts would be covered by domestic law.[20] There is no such domestic law in Afghanistan.[21]

International Human Rights Law, however, does address minimum standards of due process that apply to detention, and any domestic law or security agreement must meet those basic standards.[22] The International Covenant on Civil and Political Rights (ICCPR) provides that detention must not be arbitrary, that is, it must be based on grounds and procedures established by law, and must provide the right to challenge the detention before an impartial judicial body authorized to order a detainee's release.[23] That right must be provided within a short time of the initial detention.[24]

The United States has long taken the position that it has no international human rights obligations when acting beyond U.S. borders. The vast majority of international jurisprudence, including from the European Court of Human Rights, the International Criminal Tribunal for the former Yugoslavia (ICTY), the International Criminal Tribunal for Rwanda (ICTR), the Inter-American Court of Human Rights, the International Court of Justice and the U.N. Human Rights Committee says otherwise: that such obligations 'follow the flag' wherever a State exercises effective control in its overseas operations.[25]

As detailed below, the Detainee Review Board process does not meet minimum standards of due process required by international law.

The Obama Administration has, however, improved the process, and—at least on paper—provided some of the safeguards required under international law.

History of U.S. Detention Review Proceedings at Bagram

The U.S. military has been detaining prisoners at Bagram since May 2002. Earlier procedures, alternately called Detainee Review Boards, Unlawful Enemy Combatant Review Boards,[26] and Enemy Combatant Review Boards, involved a board of officers reviewing a detainee's status completely outside the presence of the detainee. The detainee was never told of the reasons for his detention, was never brought before the board to make a statement on his own behalf, and never had any opportunity to defend himself and argue that he did not meet the detention criteria. In these previous review procedures, no one was appointed to represent the interests of the detainee.[27] These hearings, from 2002-2008, were supposed to occur once within the first 90 days of capture, and then annually.

Beginning in April 2008, detainees were regularly notified that a board would meet to review their cases. They were

given an opportunity to appear at the initial hearing, which was held within 75 days, and to make a statement. But they were still not told of the charges or any of the evidence against them, and they were still not provided any representation or assistance.[28]

In March 2009, the Obama administration altered slightly the definition of who is detainable, and, as noted above, labeled such persons "unprivileged alien enemy belligerents" instead of "unlawful enemy combatants." As a practical matter, based on our interviews with former detainees over the years the definition does not appear to have substantially altered the scope of who is being detained. It is difficult to know for sure, however, because the U.S. government does not provide information about who is detained at Bagram and the grounds for their detention. Moreover, because detainees at Bagram have so far been denied the right of habeas corpus,[29] the grounds for their detention have not been litigated in court or made publicly available in any other forum. Given that the detainee population at Bagram has almost tripled since the definition was changed, however, it is fair to question whether the change in terminology significantly narrows the category of who is detainable.

Notably, in August 2009, U.S. Marine Corps Reserve Major General Douglas M. Stone, after investigating U.S. detention practices in Afghanistan, reportedly told senior U.S. military officials that most of the detainees held at Bagram were not dangerous and should be released.[30]

In September 2009, Secretary of Defense Robert Gates created the Combined Joint Interagency Task Force 435 (JTF 435) to control detention operations for the Defense Department in Afghanistan. JTF 435 assumed responsibility for most U.S. detention operations, including the care and custody of detainees at the Detention Facility in Parwan (DFIP), a new prison opened in December 2009 to accommodate the growing detainee population at Bagram.[31] (Parwan is the name of the province where the Bagram Air Base is located.) JTF 435 is also responsible for detainee review processes, programs for the reintegration of detainees into Afghan society, and coordination with other U.S. agencies and other participating governments for the promotion of the rule of law in Afghanistan.

Significantly, the detention of some U.S. prisoners in the initial "screening" phase of their custody at Bagram does not fall under the command of JTF 435. Captives held at what the United States calls "screening facilities" at the Bagram Air Base or elsewhere around Afghanistan are reportedly under the command of United States Joint Special Operations Command.[32] Information about these screening facilities is classified, however, and the United States government refuses to share any information about their locations or conditions.[33] Based on information reported by journalists, by the Open Society Institute,[34] and on our interviews with former detainees released in 2009, it is clear that the treatment of prisoners and detention conditions at these facilities is significantly worse than at the DFIP. Former detainees told Human Rights First in February, and previously in October and November 2010, that they were held in isolation for two weeks or more, some kept in cells that were extremely cold, were denied natural light and had difficulty sleeping because an electric light was on 24-hours-a-day in each cell. Some were also interrogated in the middle of the night, suggesting that they may have been subjected to intentional sleep disruption and deprivation.

Although Vice Admiral Harward has said that detainees are transferred out of any screening facilities after 14 days, other U.S. officials reportedly have said that detainees may be held there much longer, for up to nine weeks, if they are believed to be providing important intelligence.[35]

Such treatment could be interpreted as consistent with Appendix M of the Army Field Manual.[36] Human Rights First, along with former interrogators and intelligence officials, has expressed concerns that Appendix M may be construed to allow for the abusive treatment of detainees and called for its elimination.[37]

Because this report focuses on the hearings given to detainees after their arrival at the DFIP, it will not address

detention conditions in the screening facilities or elsewhere in detail.

Current Policy and Practice Governing U.S. Detentions in Afghanistan

Detention Facilities

Under current U.S. policy, U.S. forces have authority to detain individuals believed to be belligerents, consistent with the laws of war. Detainees may be held in segregation at classified "Special Operations Camps,"[38] including at what detainees call the "Tor Jail" or "Black Jail" on the Bagram Air Base, for up to two weeks before being transferred to the DFIP.[39] Detainees refer to this as the "Black Jail" or "Tor Jail" because it has no windows or natural light, and they cannot determine the time of day.[40] In our interviews with former detainees, seven out of 17 we interviewed said they were held in this part of the prison for longer than 14 days. All of those were prisoners initially detained before the opening of the DFIP in December 2009.

Detention Review Board: Timing & Notice

Within 60 days of a detainee's transfer to the DFIP, DoD rules require that the detainee be given an initial DRB hearing. After that hearing, the detainee should receive another DRB every six months.

Within 30 days of his scheduled DRB hearing, the detainee is supposed to be appointed a "personal representative": a U.S. military officer who is assigned to represent the detainee at the upcoming DRB.[41]

Participants in Detainee Review Board Hearings

a) DRB Members

The Detainee Review Board consists of three field grade officers who are nominated by their commanders for the post. Board members "by age, experience and temperament must be able to exercise sound judgment and have a general understanding of combat operations and the current campaign plan to assess threats in theater and further the counterinsurgency mission through their participation on each board."

To encourage their neutrality, "no board members will be among those directly involved in the detainee's capture or transfer to the DFIP."[42]

b) The Recorder

According to DoD policy, the Recorder is "a non-voting officer, preferably an officer in the Judge Advocate General Corps," meaning a military lawyer. The Recorder's role is to "present the detainee case file" to the board, reading the charges and presenting "all relevant evidence" that is "reasonably available." The Recorder also provides administrative support to the board. Although technically neutral in that the Recorder does not advocate a particular position to the board, based on our observations, the Recorder's role appears to be most like that of a prosecutor, representing the interests of the government. In each case we observed, the Recorder read the charges against the detainee to the board and summarized the basis for the U.S. military's determination that the detainee met the criteria for detention.

c) Personal Representatives

Personal Representatives (P.R.s) are not lawyers. According to DoD policy, P.R.s are given a 35-hour training course as well as weekly refresher training while serving in this position.[43] Although initially serving for just three or four months at a time, Vice Admiral Robert Harward, Commander of JTF 435, told Human Rights First during our visit in February that the P.R.'s term has been extended to one year.

According to DoD policy, the P.R. is obligated to act "in the best interests of the detainee," by "gathering and presenting information that is reasonably available in the light most favorable to the detainee." A P.R. is "bound by a non-disclosure policy not to disclose information detrimental to the detainee's case that was obtained through communications between the detainee and the personal representative." The exceptions to this non-

disclosure policy are disclosures "necessary to prevent property damage, serious bodily harm or death."

The P.R. is also "under an obligation to disclose detainee conduct that is fraudulent, and may refuse to offer evidence that he firmly believes is false, so long as such belief is grounded in an objectively reasonable assessment of the facts."

The P.R. is supposed to meet with the detainee at least twice prior to the day of the detainee's hearing.[44]

Evidence Admissible in Detainee Review Boards

a) Hearsay

Much of the evidence presented in DRBs is hearsay, and according to U.S. military officials, much of that hearsay is classified.

In an ordinary United States court of law, hearsay evidence is usually excluded, or its introduction severely restricted, because it denies the accused the opportunity to challenge the source of the evidence directly. DRB hearings, however, are based on the detainee's case file. Our discussions with members of JTF 435 and U.S. military personnel at the DFIP confirms that much of the classified evidence consists of hearsay statements provided by informants or U.S. military personnel. According to DoD policy, the case file includes "classified/intelligence reports, threat assessments, detainee transfer requests, targeting packages, disciplinary reports, observation reports, photographs, video and sound recordings, sworn/unsworn statements and character letters." The DRB may rely on such evidence and the original source of the statement or other evidence need not be brought into the hearing to testify. The DRB will not consider statements obtained by torture or through cruel, inhumane or degrading treatment. As noted above, however, it is impossible to know whether classified evidence was elicited by unlawful means.

b) Classified Evidence

Much of the hearsay evidence introduced at a DRB involves intelligence reports, which are classified. Such reports or related statements are presented in a closed session that the detainee is not allowed to attend. As a result, the detainee is not entitled to see or even obtain a summary of much of the evidence that may be used against him.

As a practical matter, these limitations, coupled with the deficiencies in representation discussed below, make it nearly impossible for the detainee to challenge that evidence or refute it with other evidence.

Moreover, although the P.R. is allowed to see the classified evidence, the P.R. cannot tell the detainee what that evidence consists of. This restriction hampers the P.R.'s ability to communicate with the detainee, to thoroughly investigate the case and to provide a meaningful defense. Although JTF 435 has assigned officers to review and declassify as much of the evidence as possible, Human Rights First was told by a declassification officer at Bagram that this was being done primarily for cases that a DRB has already recommended be transferred to Afghan authorities for prosecution. Declassification was usually not being done before the DRB hearings.

c) Witnesses

Witnesses are allowed in the DRB but often not presented. Detainees technically have the right to call witnesses if they are "reasonably available." Of the seven DRB hearings that Human Rights First has witnessed, however—four in September 2010 and three more in February 2011—not a single witness was presented by the government or by the defense. Former detainees we interviewed confirmed that witnesses were rarely present at their DRB hearings. The only witnesses that did sometimes participate in the hearing, according to former detainees, were family members or other residents of their villages, who were allowed to testify as character witnesses. According to JTF 435, out of 2688 DRB hearings held between March 6, 2010 and February 3,

2011, 1584 witnesses have been brought to the DRBs since March 2010, and another 329 have testified by telephone.

The Independence and Authority of the Detainee Review Board

The DRB is responsible for assessing two things: 1) whether the detainee has committed acts that demonstrate he is an "enemy belligerent" and 2) whether he poses a future danger to U.S. forces.

Following the hearing, the DRB can make one of three recommendations. The board can recommend that the detainee be detained for another six months, at which point he'll receive another hearing; it can recommend his release; or it can recommend that he be transferred to Afghan authorities for criminal prosecution, or for participation in a reconciliation program.

For non-Afghans (third-country nationals), the DRB can recommend transfer to a third country for criminal prosecution, participation in a reconciliation program there, or release.

The DRB does not make the final decision on the future of the detainee, however. If the DRB determines that the detainee does not meet the legal criteria for detention—that is, he did not participate in the September 11, 2001 attacks and is not part of or substantially supporting the Taliban, al Qaeda or "associated forces"[45]—then DoD policy requires that he be released. However, if the DRB determines that he meets the criteria but does not pose a continuing threat to U.S. forces, the DRB's decision may be overruled.

According to a DoD Policy Memorandum, the Commander of JTF 435 or his designee must approve the transfer or release of any detainees in Afghanistan.[46] The Commander need not accept the recommendation of the DRB as to the individual's threat level, even though the DRB has heard and considered all relevant evidence—both classified and unclassified—that is available to the military. For those detainees labeled "Enduring Security Threats," the Commander or Deputy Commander of

USFOR-A must approve the transfer or release. For non-Afghans being held at the U.S. prison in Afghanistan, the Deputy Secretary of Defense or his designee makes the final decision if the DRB recommends their transfer outside of Afghanistan.

It is not clear what criteria are used to determine who constitutes an "Enduring Security Threat" or who can be released, and why some portion of detainees recommended for transfer or release continue to be held in U.S. detention in Afghanistan.

The U.S. government has not provided the number of individuals who continue to be detained despite recommendation for release by a DRB. However, documents released following FOIA requests by the ACLU indicate that a substantial number of Afghans remain imprisoned in this status. [47]

During our visit to the DFIP, Human Rights First learned that a significant number of the approximately 41 non-Afghan detainees—the U.S. government has not said exactly how many[48]—have been recommended for release by a Detainee Review Board but remain in detention at the DFIP without explanation. When asked why these individuals have not been released, Human Rights First was told that the reason was unclear, and that the decision was being made in Washington. A State Department official emphasized that the authority lies within the Defense Department.[49] Human Rights First has made a follow-up request to the Office of Detainee Affairs for the number of non-Afghans who have been cleared for release or transfer from the DFIP yet continue to be held, and the reasons for their continued detention. As of the date of this report, Human Rights First had not received a response.

During our visit to the DFIP, Human Rights First also learned that detainees who have been recommended for release but remain imprisoned six months later must undergo another DRB proceeding, regardless of whether there is new evidence available. This subsequent DRB can recommend, based on the exact same evidence that led to the earlier DRB's recommendation for release, that the detainee remain in continued indefinite detention. Human Rights First learned that this had indeed happened, in at least one case.

The reassessments raise concerns about reliability, probity, consistency and double jeopardy.

The DRBs Do Not Provide Due Process for Detainees

"They were not answering my questions about where is the evidence in court. The Personal Representative just sat, he did not talk. He didn't do anything."

–J.I., from Khost province

The touchstone of international law is that detainees must have a meaningful way to challenge the legality of their detention. Based on the inadequacies of the DRB process set forth below, we believe that current U.S. detention policy in Afghanistan does not provide detainees the minimum level of due process required by international law.

Lack of Adequate Representation

Although international law does not explicitly provide for the right to legal counsel in administrative detention (as opposed to pre-trial criminal detention), the right to effective legal assistance has come to be considered "an essential component of the right to liberty of person."[50] For example, Principle 17 of the "Body of Principles" accompanying the ICCPR provides for detained persons to have the assistance of legal counsel. It is notable that Israel, for example, provides "unlawful combatants" captured on foreign soil the right to an attorney, who represents them in independent judicial proceedings, which include a right to appeal.[51]

The U.S. government and, in particular, officials from the Office of Detainee Affairs in the Department of Defense, have repeatedly stated that they do not believe that detainees in U.S. custody in Afghanistan have a right to legal counsel to represent them, and have insisted that the P.R. is an adequate substitute for a legal representative. Based on our observations and discussions with Defense Department officials about the P.R.s' training, background and performance, we disagree that the P.R. is a sufficient substitute.

Access to legal representatives, who prioritize client representation and are trained and encouraged to assess and respond to factual assertions and allegations of wrongdoing, are necessary for a legitimate, fair, and accurate detainee review process.

Lawyers have an obligation to respect the interests of their clients and ensure their clients' confidentiality. As the DoD rules make clear, that is not always the case with P.R.s in the DRB context. Moreover, P.R.s are not required to speak the local language or receive any language or cultural training. As a result, the detainee has little reason to trust the representative. Many of the former detainees we interviewed, all of whom had experienced a DRB, told us that they did not trust the P.R.—who to them appeared as simply another uniformed American soldier—to truly represent their interests.

Most importantly, legal counsel have been trained to demand substantive evidence to support charges being made in a fact-finding hearing, and have been trained to challenge evidence to reveal its weaknesses. Although P.R.s are supposed to receive 35 hours of training pursuant to Defense Department policy, based on our observations of their performance and discussions with Defense Department personnel, this 5-day course does not appear to be adequate.[52]

The military's response to our concerns in the past has been that these hearings are intended to be non-adversarial, and therefore legal representation is not necessary. Based on what we observed, however, the P.R.s still do not appear to understand basic functions and principles of the fact-finding process. As a result, the hearings are not bringing forth all of the relevant facts necessary for the DRB to make an informed and fair decision.

Case Examples

Gul Alai

On February 7, 2011, Human Rights First observed the case of a detainee named Gul Alai. The Recorder recited the charges and facts alleged against him, saying Gul Alai "owned a compound where IED [Improvised Explosive Device] -making material was found." The Recorder went on to say that there were no bomb-making materials found on Gul Alai, or in his home, and that Gul Alai did not test positive for explosive residue. The bomb-making material was found in the house next door to his. Nevertheless, the Recorder said, Gul Alai was "assessed to be an IED facilitator."

The detainee, a bearded man dressed in a white *shalwar kamiz*[53] and wrapped in a grey blanket, stood, his ankles shackled, to defend himself. "That's my house where I was detained," he said, speaking through a Pashto translator provided by the U.S. military. But, he added: "The other house I don't know, it doesn't belong to me."

When the Recorder asked, "You own the compound you were captured in?" The detainee answered "yes." But it was not clear whether the detainee was referring to the compound or the house, and whether the translation from English to Pashto was correct.

The Detainee Review Board president interrupted, asking: "You own the house or the compound?"

The detainee responded that he owned the house. At no point, however, did anyone present any evidence of who owned the compound or who owned the house where

explosives were found, although that was obviously a critical issue in the case. The P.R. did not demand that such evidence be presented, nor did he present any evidence himself. By the end of the public portion of the DRB hearing, it remained unclear what the detainee owned and whose weapons were found.

The P.R.'s only questions to the detainee, and the P.R.'s only statements at all in the unclassified session of the hearing, concerned whether the detainee knew his neighbors and could see over their wall, and how he had been treated by the U.S. military in the DFIP. The P.R. asked no further questions, did not introduce any evidence, and made no other statements in the unclassified portion of the hearing. The detainee's last statement was simply: "I swear I'm not a Talib[an]. I'm a farmer, I'm a gardener."

Nasrullah

In another case, a man named Nasrullah[54] was one of eight detainees captured together. The Recorder read from his case file, saying that U.S. soldiers had found seven hand grenades, one Rocket-propelled grenade (RPG) round, two magazine vests and IED weapons "in the area."

As for the detainee himself, his hands tested negative for explosive residue and his DNA was a "no hit"—meaning it did not test match DNA samples taken from the explosive materials. Still, Nasrullah had been assessed to be a Taliban fighter.

Nasrullah addressed the board:

> "I was sleeping in my house with my family and my kids and they came. They searched the house, and found weapons buried in the soil. But I didn't know they were there," Nasrullah said. "It is not my house, the owner of the house lives in the city. I am his farmer. He gave me his land to grow corn." He added: "Coalition forces when they came said the weapons are there probably the last five years. They were very old."

In Nasrullah's case, as in Gul Alai's, the Recorder did not present evidence of who owned the house where the weapons were found, the age of the weapons, or any forensic evidence that might indicate how long the weapons had been buried there. The Recorder did not even ask how long the detainee had lived in the house.

Neither did the P.R. When it was his turn to speak, the P.R. asked the detainee whether he owns any weapons. The detainee said no. The P.R. also asked Nasrullah if he knew the other people arrested with him, and what he knows about them.

Then the P.R. asked, in a typical exchange (based on the hearings we observed) between a personal representative and detainee:

P.R.: Have you ever supported the Taliban?

Nasrullah: No, never.

P.R.: If the Taliban offered you money to attack Coalition forces, would you take the offer?

Nasrullah: No, I would not.

P.R.: How has been your treatment here?

Nasrullah: I'm good with them, they are very good with me, they treat me very well.

P.R.: If released, what would you tell villagers about U.S. and coalition forces?

Nasrullah: I'm going to tell them that they were giving us rice, meat, milk, good food we never had in our life. Showers, new clothes every three days."

Although the board members asked a few more questions about how long Nasrullah had lived in the house, the P.R. said nothing more. He never presented any evidence or witnesses on Nasrullah's behalf.

Anonymous

A lack of critical evidence similarly tarnished another case Human Rights First observed on the morning of February 7. In that case, a detainee[55] was accused of planting IEDs. The Recorder said that he was seen digging along the side of the road for about 40 minutes, and that coalition forces found a weapons cache on the road. They also found medical supplies, poppy seeds used to make heroin, and wire and a bolt cutter inside the nearby compound, where the detainee was arrested. The Recorder said the detainee's hands tested positive for explosive residue.

When it was his turn to speak, the detainee said that he was only at the compound because he had been playing soccer with some other men there, then was invited to dinner at someone's home in the compound and spent the night there as a guest. He denied placing IEDs or seeing any weapons. The following is his account of when he first saw the weapons in question:

> They [Coalition forces] brought us to a location, blindfolded, then showed us the items and took our pictures with them. Other than that I've never seen these items before in my life."

Neither the Recorder nor the P.R. presented any evidence about when the detainee was tested for explosive residue—whether it was before or after he was brought to the location with the weapons, and whether he handled any of the weapons at that location before he was tested.

Instead, the P.R. asked questions such as: What did you grow on your farm? What did you study in school? Did you have religious studies there?

The P.R. introduced no evidence and no witnesses.

In fact, in no case that Human Rights First witnessed, either in February or earlier in September 2010, did the P.R. introduce any evidence or call a single witness to the events being discussed in the case in an effort to challenge the government's factual assertions, even in cases where it was obviously called for. In fact, none of the P.R.s Human Rights First has observed produced any witnesses on behalf of the detainees at all.

The deficiencies we observed in the P.R.s performance suggests that either the P.R.s were not trained or encouraged to investigate the case and look for witnesses, or they did not have the time, opportunity or resources necessary to do so.

Whatever the reason, the result is that the detainee was left to fend for himself. In each case, the detainee did nothing more than make a statement denying the charges and insisting that he does not support the Taliban. Several said they did not know why they were detained, and that residents of their village would confirm this if they were brought in as witnesses. Former detainees we interviewed said during both interrogations and at their DRB hearings they specifically asked to see the evidence against them, but they were not shown any evidence. Although the P.R. sometimes asked questions, it was often unclear to what end, other than to give the detainee an opportunity to say that he would not support the Taliban in the future and would not speak badly to his neighbors about Coalition forces. Human Rights First was left with the strong impression that the P.R.s were not sufficiently trained or experienced to present an adequate defense or assist the detainee in any meaningful way.

Our interviews with former detainees confirmed this impression.

In each interview, Human Rights First asked the detainee what specifically the P.R. did for him, both before the hearing and afterwards. In each case, the detainee said that the P.R. met with him once or twice before the hearing, but did not present any witnesses or evidence pertaining to the relevant facts or the charges alleged. In no case did the P.R. challenge evidence presented by the Recorder, or question live witnesses. At most, in some cases the P.R. arranged for family members or village elders to attend the DRB and act as a character witness for the detainee.

U.S. Army soldier stands guard next to detained Afghan men in the Arghandab valley in Kandahar province February 26, 2010.[REUTERS/Baz Ratner]

In addition, it is notable that pursuant to the military's July 2010 Policy Memorandum, the Recorder is "preferably" a trained military lawyer. Because Recorders read the charges and present the evidence against the detainee, the fact that P.R.s are not lawyers presents, at the very least, an appearance of an imbalance in the procedure, with the government benefiting from the Recorders' legal training, while the detainee, represented by a non-lawyer, does not.

Reliance on Classified Evidence, Denial of the Right to Confront Witnesses

In each case we observed, the hearing was closed after about 45 minutes for a classified session that neither we nor the detainee was allowed to observe. In the classified session, the Recorder can present documentary evidence or call witnesses that possess classified information. It is possible that the P.R. challenged the evidence presented in that classified session. However, that is impossible for us to know. It is also impossible for the detainee to know. Even assuming that the government had strong classified evidence in each case to support continued detention of the detainee, the over-reliance on classified evidence detracts from the confidence in the process that the detainee being evaluated is entitled to have.

Former detainees repeatedly told us that they did not understand why they were detained, or what was the evidence against them.

M.T.

"People say Americans are very clever people, they can go to space. But why are they being deceived by these stupid intelligence reports?"

A 51-year-old former detainee and engineer, M.T. was working with the Afghan government when he was arrested in Logar Province in June 2009. He had gone to the U.S. military base to retrieve his son, who had been seized by U.S. forces. M.T. told Human Rights First that he believes someone from his village with whom he has an ongoing land dispute gave U.S. forces a false report, because he had been advocating his rights to the land in a local court.

"They accused me that I have links with the Taliban," said M.T., who said he suffers from back, leg and eye problems since his imprisonment. M.T. said he explained to U.S. forces about the land dispute, and tribal elders from his village even went to the U.S. base to plead on his behalf, but to no avail. M.T. was imprisoned for more than a year.

M.T. was assigned a personal representative about six months after his arrest. At his first DRB, "they never told me anything more specific than that I had links with the Taliban," he said. "They would not say who gave this information. I said, 'I wish you could bring that person who said this. I could know if it was from the group we have a dispute with.' But no witnesses were brought."

About six months into his detention, MT's family was able to visit him. His nephew eventually arranged to send U.S. forces some papers that documented the land dispute.

It was only after a third hearing more than a year after his arrest, which family members attended to provide testimony on his behalf, that M.T. was released.

"In all the interrogations I was telling them one thing," he told Human Rights First. "They never had proof against me. When they finally asked my family, my family confirmed the things I was saying."

M.G.

A 25-year-old farmer and father of four, M.G. had two DRBs, about six months apart. He said that he was not shown any evidence at either one. "I said 'show me the evidence, if you don't have any, let me go.' They said they are doing their investigation to find out."

M.G. said he did not know if there was any classified evidence used against him: "I don't know, I wasn't told there was any."

He was eventually released after the P.R. arranged for relatives from his village to come and testify on his behalf at his second DRB.

J.I.

A 24-year-old arrested in July 2009 after a raid on the compound where he lived, J.I. said interrogators told him initially: "We have brought you so you should give us information about your uncle."

J.I. lived in the same compound as his uncle, who worked with a Provincial Reconstruction Team in Khost. U.S. soldiers had found an AK-47 and a pistol in his uncle's home. J.I. explained that his uncle had those weapons for self-defense, because he worked in a dangerous area near the border of Pakistan.

At his DRB, about 40 days later, J.I. was accused of making explosives.

"I said I'm a student, I'm not involved. If I were, there would be my fingerprints," he said. "Do you have any evidence?"

He was not shown any evidence, he said. "They just asked, how far were you living from your uncle?"

J.I. was detained another six months. He was interrogated only twice in that time.

At his second DRB, "the judge repeated all the old charges in court," J.I. told Human Rights First. Still, he said, "they were not answering my questions about where is the evidence." Although he had a P.R., "the P.R. just sat there, he didn't talk, he didn't do anything. The P.R. didn't help me."

Although told he would be transferred to Afghan custody within weeks, J.I. was detained by U.S. forces another six months, and given another DRB. At his third DRB, "the judge spoke to three people in my family on the phone at trial," he said. "They still did not show any documents, or any evidence, at the trial."

J.I. was released three weeks later.

T.K.

T.K., a farmer from Khost province, was detained for about five months on suspicion of being a Taliban commander. He told Human Rights First: "We have hostility within my tribe, from a long time ago, when the Russians were in Afghanistan, during jihad time. My uncle was killed, and this feud continues more than 25 years later." He believed he was detained based on false statements told to U.S. forces.

At the DFIP, Human Rights First had an opportunity to speak with a de-classification officer whose role, we were told, is to declassify evidence in connection with the DRBs. What we learned, however, is that de-classification of evidence is extremely rare because it is a cumbersome process that requires the field officer who initially classified the evidence to agree to the de-classification. The de-classification officer told us that military personnel are reluctant to de-classify such material. Instead of declassification, then, the officer at the DFIP said: "we're redacting, not de-classifying." Moreover, he said that the focus of the current effort at the DFIP is on redacting or de-classifying material for trial "after they've been referred for prosecution at the DFIP," meaning after a DRB has recommended that the detainee be referred for an Afghan prosecution at the DFIP. That redaction is not taking place before the DRB hearing, he said.

The result is that the DRBs are still making their decisions based heavily on classified information that the detainee never sees and can never challenge. The detainee therefore reasonably believes he is being detained by U.S. authorities based on secret evidence that he has no reason to trust. While most biometric evidence is not classified, according to members of JTF 435, informant evidence, which is far less reliable, is classified. This is particularly a problem in Afghanistan, where longstanding tribal, family and land disputes provide fertile ground for false accusations.

Repeatedly, we were told by former detainees we interviewed that they believed they were detained by U.S. forces for months or years based on false information that the detainee was never allowed to see or challenge.

The problem of Afghans deliberately providing U.S. forces with misinformation has been acknowledged by U.S. commanders in Afghanistan.

Lt. Col. David Womack, a battalion commander, explained in a recent news report that villagers often provide false information to U.S. forces, naming rival tribes as Taliban collaborators. In one incident in Paktika province, villagers reported that the Taliban had built a road near their village. In fact, another tribe had built the road to harvest timber. "The other villagers blamed the Taliban to get the coalition to target those guys," Colonel Womack told *The New York Times*.[56]

The problem of Afghans providing U.S. forces false information against rival tribes or other enemies has similarly been noted by other organizations researching night raids, civilian casualties and detention by U.S. and NATO forces in Afghanistan.[57]

It is impossible to know precisely how many false tips have led to the imprisonment of innocent Afghans because such "intelligence" is classified. However, the large number of Afghans detained for long periods of time and eventually released without charge,[58] the frequency of civilian casualties based on misinformed targeting,[59] and the longstanding tribal conflicts and land disputes in many regions of Afghanistan suggest that U.S. actions based on false intelligence is a major problem. Indeed, one former detainee we interviewed estimated that 80 percent of the population of Khost province, where he lives, is involved in a personal or family feud that could motivate false reports to Coalition forces.

The U.S. military has a legitimate need to protect intelligence sources and methods. However, based on our conversations with former detainees, defense lawyers and human rights organizations in Afghanistan, we also understand that in the contentious environment of Afghanistan, false accusations against members of rival tribes or based on longstanding family or land disputes are common. The U.S. military must do more to ensure that the detainee can see and challenge the evidence against him. Redacting the names of informants and providing summaries of the classified evidence could substantially improve the fairness of the process, as it does in U.S. federal courts by use of the Classified Information Procedures Act (CIPA).

The heavy reliance on secret evidence to determine whether the detainee meets the criteria for continued detention is unacceptable and does not meet the minimum requirements of due process. The right of an accused to confront the witnesses against him has come to be considered a basic right of due process. Although we recognize that the Sixth Amendment right in the U.S. Constitution does not apply to DRB hearings, which are not criminal proceedings, we nonetheless believe that the government's continued heavy reliance on hearsay evidence and secret classified evidence denies the detainee a meaningful right to defend himself.

Human Rights First believes that denying detainees this right is counterproductive to the U.S. mission in Afghanistan, in that it encourages hostility toward U.S. forces from Afghan detainees and their relatives and neighbors. Repeatedly, we were told by former detainees we interviewed that they believed they were imprisoned based on false information that they were not allowed to challenge, and that in the view of their families and communities, the United States is arbitrarily detaining people based on false intelligence. Such actions create a

negative perception of U.S. forces that threatens to undermine the progress made by the reduction in civilian casualties and U.S. civilian assistance to improve basic services.[60]

Significantly, an ABC News/Washington Post poll released in December 2010 found that Afghans' support for U.S. military forces declined in 2010, coinciding with the significant increase in arrests that year.[61]

The DRBs Lack Final Authority to Order a Detainee's Release

As noted earlier, the Commander of JTF 435 or his designee must approve all transfers or releases recommended by the DRB; the board itself, which personally reviewed all of the evidence, does not have that authority. For non-Afghans being held at the U.S. prison in Afghanistan, the Deputy Secretary of Defense or his designee makes the final decision.

The result is that even if the DRB determines that a detainee does not pose a threat to U.S. forces, he may continue to be detained, without explanation. The standards guiding these final decisions are not public, nor has the U.S. government made available specific information on releases or transfers that would allow us to determine how frequently the DRB's recommendation is overruled.

That the review board lacks final authority over the detainee's fate represents a serious shortfall in due process. The ICCPR provides that anyone deprived of liberty should have the right to proceedings before an independent court with the power to order his release.[62] In the case of the DRB, the board does not have that power. This leaves the process open to arbitrary delays and the possibility of political interference and undermines both the legitimacy of the board's proceedings and the ability of the detainee to meaningfully challenge his detention.

The Enduring Problem of Third-Party Nationals

During our visit to the Bagram Air Base in February, Human Rights First learned that at least a dozen non-

Afghans imprisoned at the DFIP have been recommended
for release by a DRB but remain imprisoned without
explanation. Neither military nor State Department
officials were able to explain to us what or who was
obstructing their release, or for what reasons they were
being held. Without such information, this seems to be a
clear case of arbitrary detention.[63]

Lack of Compensation for Wrongful Detention, Theft or Damage to Property

> *"They searched my house so aggressively....they stuck the sacks with the knife in the search, damaged all the grains, mixed up the different grains. It was a loss worth about $5000....There was no apology, no compensation at all. I told them that you guys destroyed my grain, I had big losses. But nobody cared."*
>
> **–Tawab, a farmer from Kunar province**

The detainees we interviewed all said that they were not compensated for what they viewed as a wrongful imprisonment. In some cases an individual soldier would apologize to the detainee, but the detainees rarely received an official apology and never received compensation upon their release. This problem was compounded in cases where U.S. or accompanying Afghan military officers damaged the detainee's home or other property at the time of arrest.

T.K., a farmer in his 30s from Khost province told us: "Jewelry, necklaces, earrings. The Afghan soldiers took all this. Even body spray, deodorant. I have not gotten it back."

T., a farmer in his 50s from Kunar province, told us that U.S. soldiers, while searching his home in the middle of the night, slashed with knives large sacks of grain he was storing, causing the grain to spill out and mix on the floor. T. had intended to sell the different grains in the local market, but could not sell them after they'd been mixed together. He estimated the damages cost at least $5000. "There was no apology, no compensation at all," he said. "I told the soldiers, 'you guys destroyed my grain, I have big losses,' but nobody cared." He said he was too afraid of local authorities or U.S. officials to formally seek a remedy from the U.S. military.

M.G., a detainee from Khost province, was arrested in March 2010, when his home was raided around midnight. U.S. and Afghan soldiers entered and searched the house. "They took money from the house," he said, including about $700 in compensation that the family had received after his brother, who was working for U.S. forces, was killed. "They also took some gold, and a passport that belonged to my nephew," he said. "When they released me, I asked for these things. I was told to go home and they would be returned to me. They never were."

The Constitution of Afghanistan provides that "[a]ny person suffering undue harm by government action is entitled to compensation." Although this provision may not bind the United States, Afghans have reasonably been led to believe that they are entitled to compensation when they suffer at the hands of the authorities in charge.[64] In addition, the ICCPR provides that "Anyone who has been the victim of unlawful arrest or detention shall have an enforceable right to compensation."[65]

Although we recognize the difficulty of U.S. authorities determining who should be compensated for mistaken imprisonment, U.S. policy acknowledges the importance of at least compensating damages caused by U.S. soldiers.[66] Such compensation for property damaged or stolen during arrests does not appear to be happening in a systematic manner.

General Stanley McChrystal acknowledged this problem in 2009 and recommended that a new compensation system be developed, noting that "appropriate measures to ensure accountability and recognition of the importance of Afghan life and property can help mitigate public anger over the incident."[67] We are not aware of any progress having been made based on this recommendation.[68]

Transition of Detention Authority to Afghan Control

"I told him, on what basis are you handing us over? Afghan
officials will ask us for money, and we don't have money."

–J.I., from Khost, after 3 DRBs, turned over to Afghan authorities

In 2005, the Afghan and U.S. governments entered into a bilateral agreement that set forth conditions for the transfer of Afghan detainees in U.S. custody to the Afghan government. According to the U.S. Embassy, this "Joint Declaration on Strategic Partnership" allows for the "gradual transfer of Afghan detainees to the exclusive custody and control of the Afghan government." The United States has pledged "to assist Afghanistan in capacity building, including infrastructure, and to provide training, as appropriate."

More recently, in December, William Lietzau, Deputy Assistant Secretary for Detainee Policy, stated that the JTF 435 "will begin to transition detention operations at the DFIP to the Government of Afghanistan in January 2011," and that the speed of the transition will depend on "operational conditions, Afghan judicial capacity, and whether the GIRoA [Government of Afghanistan] is fully trained, equipped, and able to perform its detention, prosecution, and incarceration responsibilities in accordance with its international obligations and Afghan law."[69]

Lietzau also stated:

> Consistent with a memorandum of understanding signed by the pertinent Afghan ministries on January 9, 2010, it is expected that once the DFIP is transferred to the GIRoA, it will become part of a larger Afghan Justice Center in Parwan, which is intended to become Afghanistan's central location for the pre-trial detention, prosecution, and post-

trial incarceration of individuals who commit crimes against Afghan security.

The first Afghan trial was held at the DFIP with Afghan judges, prosecutors and defense counsel on June 8, 2010. By February 2011, more than 50 Afghan trials had been held at the DFIP. According to Lietzau, eventually, "individuals who are convicted and sentenced in the Afghan trials at the DFIP will serve their sentences in those Afghan-controlled DFIP housing units."

Documents provided to Human Rights First by JTF 435 during our recent visit to Bagram indicate that the transition is now expected to be complete by 2014, which is also the target date for the United States to withdraw its troops from Afghanistan. The United States has not said, however, that it will relinquish its right to detain prisoners in Afghanistan after that date. On the contrary, JTF 435 Commander Robert Harward said in January that he expects the U.S. will continue to detain about 80 of the current prisoners now at the DFIP either because they are third-country nationals or because the U.S. has decided that they are too dangerous to release or to transfer to the Afghan government for trial.[70]

Human Rights First had an opportunity to observe only one Afghan trial held at the DFIP during our February visit. Although this was insufficient to allow us to draw conclusions about progress toward the transition of detention authority to Afghan control, the trial raised serious concerns about the capacity of the Afghan justice system to provide detainees the minimum international legal requirements of due process. We hope to have an

An Afghan man detained by U.S. Marines at base in Talibjan, November 7, 2010. [REUTERS/Finbarr O'Reilly]

opportunity to observe more of these Afghan trials as the United States develops its training and mentoring program at the DFIP.

Unlike the DRBs, the detainee in the Afghan trial we observed was represented by a defense attorney. Still, as with the DRBs we witnessed, neither the prosecutor nor the defense attorney introduced any witnesses or presented any substantive evidence at trial.

The only evidence presented at the brief trial, which lasted about a half-hour, was a propaganda video that the prosecutor played on his laptop for the judge. From his brief description, we understood that it showed weapons being used, accompanied by Islamic music, apparently for the cause of Jihad. Neither the detainee nor any observers in the room could see the video, however. The detainee's lawyer objected that such videos can be easily purchased in the open market, and that the prosecutor had not indicated where the video came from.

Moreover, as both the defense lawyer and one of the three judges presiding over the trial pointed out, the video had no evident connection to the defendant. Neither he nor any of this family members appeared in the video,

and it was not found on or anywhere near the defendant or his home.

The prosecutor explained that he was showing the video simply to explain how weapons recovered from a mosque where the defendant was arrested could be used.

As in the DRBs, at the trial the defendant was given an opportunity to speak. A 24-year-old farmer named Kamal, who wore a coffee-colored *shalwar kamiz* and beat-up sneakers with the backs folded down, stood and explained that at the age of 15, he had been diagnosed with a heart condition, which prevented him from walking very much, let alone fighting. He said he was arrested last summer after he left the local mosque with his uncle, who had encountered some friends of his on the road. His uncle instructed him to return to the mosque with his friends and guard them with an AK-47. He said he reluctantly agreed, and when a helicopter arrived with Coalition forces to raid the mosque, the men fled and he hid in the mosque. His uncle was killed in the firefight that followed, and he was captured.

Kamal was accused of participating in an armed assault and of Taliban membership. He had already been imprisoned for seven months.

At the end of the hearing, the three judges left the room. After about 10 minutes, they returned and announced the verdict. The defendant was acquitted of the charge of participating in an armed assault, because there was no evidence that he assaulted anyone or fired any weapons, the chief judge said. He was convicted, however, of membership with an enemy organization, and sentenced to five years in prison. Yet there was no evidence presented at the trial demonstrating his membership.

The only "evidence" presented was a statement by the prosecutor that "facts received from NDS [Afghanistan's National Directorate of Security] shows that he was involved in destructive activities in the region." The prosecutor never presented any of those facts at the trial, however. Instead, he said only: "NDS gave us this information. Why would they provide us with wrong information? They have no reason to."

While we recognize that the Afghan justice system is based on a civil law system that is less adversarial than ours, there was no indication that any of the attorneys or judges involved had thoroughly investigated the case and produced evidence to support or challenge the charges.

Joint Task Force 435 says it is working with the Afghan government to provide training and mentoring to Afghan judges, prosecutors and defense lawyers conducting these trials. According to the Defense Department, such training has been taking place since at least June 2010, when the first Afghan trial was held on the U.S. military base. U.S. military personnel were present at the trial we observed and had supposedly advised the Afghan lawyers and judges. Still, the conduct of the trial we observed was not encouraging, and raised serious questions about whether the United States wants to be effectively putting its stamp of approval on trials that do not meet the basic minimum requirements of due process.

While in Afghanistan, we had an opportunity to speak to Afghan defense lawyers and directors of Afghan criminal defense organizations. They all expressed serious concerns that defense lawyers in Afghanistan are frequently not allowed to act independently and in the best interests of their clients. Moreover, all remain very concerned about pervasive corruption in the Afghan judicial system, with judges routinely seeking bribes to supplement their meager monthly government incomes. Defense lawyers also complained that many judges lack the necessary legal education to properly do their jobs, and that many were appointed due to political, ethnic or tribal connections, rather than based on merit.

Former detainees we interviewed expressed a similar lack of confidence in the Afghan justice system. Some told us that when U.S. officials informed them that they could be transferred from U.S. to Afghan custody for trial, they were afraid that the only way they would ever be released is if

they or their families paid bribes to Afghan officials—which they could not afford to do.

The concerns we heard were all consistent with those expressed in several recent reports issued by other non-governmental organizations, by the United Nations, the Congressional Research Service and even the U.S. State Department.

Last year, for example, the International Crisis Group reported that despite repeated promises over the last nine years by the government of Afghanistan to improve its justice system with the help of international donors, "the majority of Afghans still have little or no access to judicial institutions," the public has "no confidence in the formal justice sector" and Afghan judges and prosecutors remain "highly susceptible to corruption." [71]

The Congressional Research Service in November 2010 released a report reaching similar conclusions about the dismal state of the Afghan justice system. [72]

A United Nations report in 2009 likewise noted "systematic weaknesses" in the Afghan formal justice system, concluded that "Afghanistan's legal and regulatory frameworks are inadequate and do not include critical rights or guidance to authorities," that "competing concepts of justice" lead to "a presumption of guilt that permeates the criminal justice system," and that "impunity, corruption and weak oversight mechanisms enable arbitrary detention practices to continue uncorrected." [73]

The United States' 2010 country report on human rights in Afghanistan, released in April 2011, similarly notes that although Afghan law prohibits arbitrary arrest and detention, "both remained serious problems." In addition, "official impunity was pervasive"; prosecutors filed indictments in cases even where "there was a reasonable belief that no crime actually was committed"; Afghan trial procedures "rarely met internationally accepted standards"; and, the State Department found, the Afghan judiciary "often was underfunded, understaffed, and subject to political influence and pervasive corruption." [74]

Human Rights First supports the United States' interest in helping the Afghan government to improve the trials provided for national security detainees, not least because it will help facilitate the transfer of detention operations from the U.S. to the Afghan government. Helping the Afghan government meet basic minimum standards of due process, however, will require a lasting commitment on the part of the U.S. government, working in coordination with other donor nations. Given that the training and mentoring responsibilities in these cases at this time appear to rest almost entirely on the Department of Defense, it is not clear what kind of commitment the U.S. government will continue to make after U.S. military forces are withdrawn. We urge the government to make the development of a legitimate justice system a top priority, not only as it transitions its military forces out of Afghanistan, but also as a key element of helping Afghanistan develop a stable society.

The State Department's Office of Inspector General, reporting on Rule of Law (ROL) programs in Afghanistan last year, noted the "direct connection between the lack of a workable system of governance and the national security of the United States…. Confidence that the government can provide a fair and effective justice system is an important element in convincing war-battered Afghans to build their future in a democratic system rather than reverting to one dominated by terrorists, warlords, and narcotics traffickers. Without ROL the country cannot progress no matter what contributions are made by outsiders."[75]

We agree. An effective and trusted justice system is critical to the future stability of Afghanistan. It is therefore also critical to U.S. national security interests in the region.

Recommendations

Human Rights First makes the following recommendations to the United States government for how to improve the DRB process and support a successful transition of detention operations to Afghan control.

To the Department of Defense

Improve the Quality of Detainee Representation

- Provide detainees with legal representation.

- If legal representation is not possible at this time, improve the training provided to P.R.s to ensure that they understand the importance of demanding and challenging the evidence upon which the government's charges against the detainees are based.

- If legal representation for each detainee is not possible, make defense lawyers available at the DFIP who can advise P.R.s on how to investigate cases and defend detainees.

- Increase the number of P.R.s so that each one can spend more time investigating each case and preparing each detainee's defense. As of February 2011, there were only 15 P.R.s available to represent about 1700 detainees. This is insufficient to allow them to investigate each case, let alone prepare a meaningful defense.

- Provide access and funding for Afghan defense lawyers to work with P.R.s at the DFIP. Afghan lawyers can help explain to detainees the charges against them, the role of the P.R.s and the purpose of and opportunities presented by the detainee's upcoming DRB. Involving Afghan lawyers in this way will also bolster U.S. efforts to

improve the handling of national security cases by the Afghan justice system.

- Provide basic language and cultural training to P.R.s to improve their ability to relate to the detainee, to win his confidence, and to investigate his case.

- As part of their cultural training, P.R.s should be trained specifically to question detainees about personal, family or tribal feuds that may be going on in the detainee's village or province and might have led someone to provide false information against him to U.S. forces.

Increase Transparency of the DRB Process

- Declassify as much evidence as possible, by using carefully limited redaction and providing summaries of classified evidence when the evidence itself cannot be produced. This should be done before the evidence is used in the DRBs, not only for Afghan trials. The Classified Information Procedures Act, which has allowed prosecutors to successfully prosecute cases involving classified evidence in U.S. federal courts, provides useful guidance on how the DRBs can use classified evidence while minimizing any compromise of due process.

- Inform the detainee of his future DRB hearing within 14 days of his transfer to the DFIP. Current policies require detainees to be told of the basis for their internment at that time, but do not require informing detainees that they will have a hearing where they may contest the charges against them.

- Ensure that interrogators share with P.R.s any statements or evidence they have obtained, both inculpatory and exculpatory.

- End the practice of subjecting detainees recommended for release by one DRB to a second DRB, in the absence of substantial new evidence that is likely to alter the outcome.

- Ensure that all detainees recommended for release are actually released expeditiously. For those, such as third-country nationals, who are not released despite a release recommendation, explain the reasons to the detainee. In all cases, make every effort possible not to hold the detainee for more than a month after a DRB has recommended his release.

- Report publicly on how many detainees are being held after a recommendation for release or transfer from a DRB, the length of detention following that recommendation, and the reason for anyone held longer than one month after a DRB's recommendation for release or transfer.

- Make public the criteria used by the DRBs for continued detention of detainees, including the criteria used to determine who is an "Enduring Security Threat."

- Make public the criteria used by the JTF 435 Commander and by the Deputy Secretary of Defenseto determine whether or not to follow the recommendation of the DRB.

- Make public the report prepared by Major General Douglas Stone in 2009 analyzing U.S. detention operations in Afghanistan and recommending reforms.

To the Department of Defense and the Department of State

Continue to Support Improvements to the Afghan Justice System

- Focus national security case training and mentoring of Afghan judges, prosecutors and defense attorneys on the need to thoroughly investigate and gather substantive evidence.

- Train Afghan judges and lawyers about the importance of presenting evidence in open court and challenging the evidence presented as a critical part of the fact-finding process.

- Begin to transition the U.S. military-led training and mentoring effort on national security cases to a civilian-led training effort, so that such training and mentoring continues regardless of the presence of the U.S. military in Afghanistan.

Conclusion

"The laws and Constitution are designed to survive, and remain in force, in extraordinary times. Liberty and security can be reconciled; and in our system they are reconciled within the framework of the law."

–Boumedienne v. Bush[76]

After many years of completely denying detainees in Afghanistan the opportunity to defend themselves against arbitrary detention, the United States government has finally implemented a hearing process that allows detainees to hear the charges against them and to make a statement in their own defense. While a significant improvement, these new hearings fall short of minimum standards of due process required by international law.

In imprisoning people indefinitely without meaningful independent review, the United States is depriving these detainees of their liberty, casting suspicions upon them in their community and often depriving extended Afghan families of their primary breadwinner and source of protection and support. Because imprisoning suspected insurgents is such a serious matter for the men themselves, for their families and for their communities, it is incumbent upon the United States government to create a mechanism that ensures that those it is holding are dangerous insurgents and not innocent Afghans.

Only by providing detainees in Afghanistan an opportunity to defend themselves in a meaningful manner with the assistance of legal counsel and the opportunity to confront witnesses and the evidence against them can the United States ensure that it is imprisoning the right people. Moreover, only by providing real due process, and demonstrating by example what due process requires, can the United States expect to win the trust and respect of the Afghan people, who see themselves as vulnerable to U.S. military power.

The death of Osama bin Laden is likely to increase pressure on the Obama Administration to withdraw U.S. troops from Afghanistan soon. As the United States draws down its military involvement, it should shift some of those resources toward a civilian effort to improve the rule of law in Afghanistan.

The United States' goal of helping Afghanistan improve its justice system is an important and laudable one. In the long term, it will help stabilize the country by encouraging Afghans' respect for their government and trust in their government institutions to protect them. Improving the administration of justice in national security cases will also directly help to ensure that violent insurgents remain incarcerated and cannot threaten Afghan national security. Given the sorry state of the Afghan justice system after decades of war and entrenched corruption, however, this goal is necessarily a long-term one. Even after the United States withdraws the bulk of its troops from Afghanistan, ongoing support for its fledgling justice system will be necessary, and critical to the country's stable development. Human Rights First urges the United States government to take a long-term view of the problem and to commit to civilian assistance for Afghan judges, lawyers and legal institutions far into the future.

Timeline of Detention Events in Afghanistan

October 7, 2001	U.S. Operation Enduring Freedom begins as an international armed conflict. Taliban falls in November.
November 24, 2001	U.S. begins detention operations to screen detainees from as far away as Central Africa and South Asia in fight against Al Qaeda. Prisoners are held in makeshift pens of razor wire.
May 2002	The Bagram Collection Point, located at the Bagram Airfield, a former soviet military base north of Kabul, becomes the primary detention facility for U.S. forces in Afghanistan.
June 2002	President Hamid Karzai is elected, and then appointed by the Loya Jirga. The conflict is now an internal, non-international armed conflict.
Summer 2002	U.S. starts Detention Review Boards at Bagram, comprised of about 10 U.S. military personnel, to screen detainees. Detainees are not present or notified of the proceedings, which are classified. U.S. claims Geneva Conventions do not apply.
December 3, 2002	Two Bagram prisoners found shackled to ceiling of jail, murdered. In 2005 and 2006, five soldiers plead guilty; one is convicted. Longest sentence is five months.
2002-2004	Widespread reports emerge of torture and abuse at Bagram.
September 2004	President George W. Bush halts transfer of prisoners from Bagram to Guantanamo to avoid U.S. federal court review. Bagram population begins to increase.
Summer 2005	Pentagon institutes new Enemy Combatant Review Boards (ECRBs), comprised of five officers. Prisoners still have no right to attend hearing, to a lawyer or other representative, or to review or dispute evidence.
December 2005	Congress passes Detainee Treatment Act of 2005, ostensibly banning prisoner abuse.
September 2006	Appendix M is added to the Army Field Manual to allow combination of isolation, sleep deprivation and other techniques that could be interpreted as allowing abusive interrogations of high-value detainees. President Obama makes the Army Field Manual the single standard for interrogation shortly after his inauguration.
February 2007	Pentagon ends ECRBs and creates new three-member Unlawful Enemy Combatant Review Boards (UECRBs). New procedure does not provide detainees with any more rights.
April 2008	Detainees for the first time receive notice of when their cases will be reviewed and may appear and speak at initial hearing, without legal or other representation. Detainees may provide written statements for subsequent six-month reviews.
June 2008	Supreme Court rules Guantanamo detainees are entitled to challenge their detention in federal court.

January 2009	Barack Obama is sworn in as president of the United States, signs three executive orders aimed at improving U.S. detention practices.
February 20, 2009	Justice Department announces in federal court that it opposes habeas corpus for Bagram detainees. D.C. Circuit Court of Appeals accepts the government's position in decision on May 21, 2010.
March 2009	President Obama unveils new U.S. strategy for Afghanistan and Pakistan and claims authority to detain "unprivileged enemy belligerents." To be detainable, individuals now must have "substantially" supported the Taliban, al Qaeda or associated forces.
July 2, 2009	Department of Defense (DoD) issues memo detailing new detention review procedure at Bagram, providing detainees right to a personal representative (not a lawyer), the right to attend hearings and challenge evidence. Detainee has no right to review classified evidence.
August 29, 2009	U.S. Marine Corps General Douglas Stone, who revamped detention operations in Iraq, reports that nearly 2/3 of detainees at Bagram pose no threat to U.S. or Afghanistan and should be released. Recommends U.S. shift focus from detention to rehabilitation.
September 2009	Combined Joint Interagency Task Force 435 (JTF 435) is created to control detention operations in Afghanistan. UECRBs begin to be replaced by new Detainee Review Boards (DRBs). At DRBs, military lawyers called "Recorders" present the case against the detainee to a three-officer board. Detainees are represented by non-lawyer officers called "Personal Representatives."
November 2009	Reports surface that mistreatment of detainees continues at a "black jail" at the Bagram Air Base.
December 2009	Bagram prisoners are transferred to new $60 million Detention Facility in Parwan (DFIP), also on the Bagram Air Base.
December 2009	President Obama increases troops in Afghanistan to 100,000 as part of surge.
June 2010	First Afghan trial is held at the DFIP.
July 2010	DoD issues new memo detailing DRB procedures.
March 2011	Detainee population at DFIP reaches 1700.

Endnotes

[1] Memorandum from General David Petraeus, Commander of the International Security Forces and United States Forces in Afghanistan, to members of NATO and United States Forces (Aug. 1, 2010), *available at* http://smallwarsjournal.com/documents/comisafcoinguidance.pdf.

[2] UNITED STATES FORCES-AFGHANISTAN (USFOR-A), INITIAL ASSESSMENT OF THE COMMANDER OF THE NATO INTERNATIONAL SECURITY ASSISTANCE FORCES – AFGHANISTAN (COMISAF), Annex F, p. F-1 (2009) [hereinafter COMISAF Assessment].

[3] Statement, Obama for America, Statement on Supreme Court Decision (June 12, 2008), *available at* http://my.barackobama.com/page/community/post/samgrahamfelsen/gG5Gz5.

[4] Memorandum from Robert Harward, Vice Admiral, U.S. Navy, Deputy Commander, Det. Operations, U.S. Dep't of Def., to U.S. Military Forces Conducting Detention Operations in Afghanistan (July 19, 2010) [hereinafter MEMORANDUM] (on file with author).

[5] International Covenant on Civil and Political Rights, art. 9(2) and (4), *entered into force* Mar. 23, 1976, S. Exec. Rep. No. 102-23 (1992). 999 U.N.T.S. 171 [hereinafter ICCPR].

[6] Jelena Pejic, *Procedural Principles and Safeguards for Internment/Administrative Detention in Armed Conflict and Other Situations of Violence*, 87 Int'l Rev. of the Red Cross 375, 388 (2005).

[7] Human Rights First produced three previous reports on Afghanistan: HUMAN RIGHTS FIRST, ARBITRARY JUSTICE (2008); HUMAN RIGHTS FIRST, UNDUE PROCESS (2009); and HUMAN RIGHTS FIRST , FIXING BAGRAM (2009) (incorporating the earlier 2009 report, UNDUE PROCESS).

[8] Recent polls show that support for U.S. troops in Afghanistan is already slipping. An ABC News/BBC/ARD/Washington Post Poll released in December 2010 found that Afghan views of U.S. forces have become more negative over the last five years. In one measure, the poll of nearly 1700 adults across Afghanistan found that just 43 percent of Afghans expressed a favorable opinion of the United States, down eight points from the year before, and only 32 percent rate the U.S. performance in Afghanistan positively. This is about half the rate of positive responses received in both categories in 2005. *See Afghanistan: Where Things Stand: Afghan Views Worsen as Setbacks Counter U.S. Progress in Helmand*, ABC NEWS/BBC/ARD/WASH. POST, Dec. 6, 2010 [hereinafter Poll].

[9] The New York Times recently reported that Afghan villagers "often provide dubious information" to U.S. forces, "identifying rival tribes as Taliban collaborators" in the hopes that U.S. forces will target their rivals. Ray Rivera, *In an Afghan Village, Living in Fear of Both Sides*, N.Y.Times, April 23, 2011.

[10] Tom Bowman et al., *U.S. General Urges Release of Bagram's Detainees* (NPR radio broadcast Aug. 20, 2009).

[11] Interview with William Lietzau, Deputy Assistant Secretary of Defense for Detainee Policy in Wash., D.C. (Mar. 30, 2011). The Associated Press reported in April 2011 that the number of prisoners at Bagram had grown to about 1900. Kimberly Dozier, *AP Exclusive: Terror suspects held weeks in secret*, ASSOCIATED PRESS, Apr. 8, 2011.

[12] Significantly, the Combatant Status Review Tribunals provided for review by a federal appeals court, which the process at Bagram does not. The Supreme Court in *Boumediene v. Bush*, 553 U.S. 723, 798 (2008) ruled that the CSRT was not an adequate substitute for habeas corpus, but the Court has not had an opportunity to rule on whether Bagram detainees are entitled to the writ. The Boumediene Court also acknowledged that the CSRT more generally raised significant due process concerns, for "even when all the parties involved in this process act with diligence and in good faith, there is considerable risk of error in the tribunal's findings of fact....And given that the consequence of error may be detention of persons for the duration of hostilities that may last a generation or more, this is a risk too significant to ignore."

[13] This statement was translated from Dari by an interpreter working for the court.

[14] *See* Brief of Amici Curiae in support of the Petitioners at 5, *Rahman v. Gates*, No. 10-320 (D.C. Dist. Mar. 28, 2011) (citing HJC 3239/02 *Marab v. IDF Commander in the West Bank* IsrSC 57(2) 349, ¶ 9 [2003]("[W]e should do our best to interpret the existing laws in a manner that is consistent with the new realities and the principles of international humanitarian law.")).

[15] Although the U.S. military has claimed that providing judicial review to detainees at Bagram would be impracticable in part due to the large number of detainees, it is noteworthy that the Israel Defense Forces in operations on the West Bank in May 2002 seized nearly 7000 suspected enemy combatants, quickly processed and released over 5000, and gave the remaining 1600 suspects access to defense counsel and to independent

courts within a matter of weeks. *See* Brief of Amici Curiae in support of the Petitioners at 5, *Rahman v. Gates*, No. 10-320 (D.C. Dist. Mar. 28, 2011) (citing HJC 3239/02 *Marab v. IDF Commander in the West Bank* IsrSC 57(2) 349, ¶ 1 [2003]).

[16] Diplomatic Note No. 202 dated Sept. 26, 2002, Exhibit 2 to Declaration of Colonel Charles A. Tennison, First Amended Petition for Writ of Habeas Corpus, *Maqaleh v. Gates*, 1:06-cv-01669, filed Sept. 15, 2008.

[17] Accommodation Consignment Agreement for Lands and Facilities at Bagram Airfield Between Afghanistan and the United States of America, dated Sept. 26, 2006, Exhibit 1(A) to Declaration of Colonel Charles A. Tennison, First Amended Petition for Writ of Habeas Corpus, *Maqaleh v. Gates*, 1:06-cv-01669, filed Sept. 15, 2008.

[18] Respondents' Memorandum Regarding the Government's Detention Authority Relative to Detainees Held at Guantanamo Bay, In re: Guantanamo Bay Detainee Litigation, 05-0763 (JDB), 05-1646 (JDB), 05-2378 (JDB).

[19] *See* Geneva Convention (III) Relative to the Treatment of Prisoners of War, art. 21, Aug. 12, 1949, 75 U.N.T.S. 135; Geneva Convention (IV) Relative to the Protection of Civilian Persons in Time of War, art. 42, Aug. 12, 1949, 75 U.N.T.S. 287.

[20] Pejic, *supra* note 6, at 389.

[21] The Fourth Geneva Convention, addressing the rights of civilians interned during wartime, presents the closest analogy to the current situation of a non-international armed conflict where the United States is detaining unprivileged belligerents. The ICRC has interpreted GC IV as requiring review by an independent board with the authority to order a detainee's release. *See* THE GENEVA CONVENTIONS OF 12 AUGUST 1949: COMMENTARY, VOL. IV, GENEVA CONVENTION RELATIVE TO THE PROTECTION OF CIVILIAN PERSONS IN TIME OF WAR, 260-62 (Jean Pictet, ed., 1958); *see also* Chris Jenks & Eric Talbot Jensen, *Indefinite Detention under the Laws of War*, XXII STANFORD LAW & POL'Y REV. (forthcoming 2011) (citing Geneva Convention (IV), art. 72):

Accused persons shall have the right to present evidence necessary to their defence and may, in particular, call witnesses. They shall have the right to be assisted by a qualified advocate or counsel of their own choice, who shall be able to visit them freely and shall enjoy the necessary facilities for preparing the defence.

Failing a choice by the accused, the Protecting Power may provide him with an advocate or counsel. When an accused person has to meet a serious charge and the Protecting Power is not functioning, the Occupying Power, subject to the consent of the accused, shall provide an advocate or counsel.

Accused persons shall, unless they freely waive such assistance, be aided by an interpreter, both during preliminary investigation and during the hearing in court. They shall have the right at any time to object to the interpreter and to ask for his replacement.

Jenks and Talbot also recognize the relevance and virtue of applying such protections, designed for criminal prosecution, to detention determinations, noting that "the rights are essentially the same as would be available during administrative proceedings within the U.S. military." Comparison of process due to detainees and that due within the U.S. military is apt. The due process provisions of Geneva Conventions III and IV establish minimum requirements, but otherwise are founded on a "golden rule" principle that the detaining authority should provide to detainees the same process that it would provide to its own military or civilians under its domestic law. *See, e.g.*, Geneva Convention (III), *supra* note 19, arts. 102, 106; Geneva Convention (IV), *supra* note 19, arts. 117, 126.

[22] *See* Pejic *supra* note 6; *See also* UNDUE PROCESS, *supra* note 7.

[23] ICCPR, *supra* note 5, art. 9(2), (4).

[24] *See* Pejic *supra* note 6, at 379-83.

[25] The European Court of Human Rights establishes binding precedent for the 47 member States of the Council of Europe. The ICTY and ICTR are international tribunals established by the U.N. Security Council to adjudicate crimes in former Yugoslavia and Rwanda, respectively. The Inter-American Court of Human Rights issues judgments on the American Convention on Human Rights and is part of the human rights enforcement mechanism of the Organization of American States, of which the United States is part, although the United States has signed, but not ratified the Convention and does not accept the jurisdiction of the Inter-American Court. The International Court of Justice is the judicial arm of the United Nations. The Human Rights Committee issues non-binding interpretations of the ICCPR for that treaty's 167 States party, including the United States.

[26] FIXING BAGRAM, *supra* note 7, at 46.

[27] Jeffrey Bovarnick, *Detainee Review Boards in Afghanistan: From Strategic Liability to Legitimacy*, ARMY LAW, June 2010, at 9, 18.

[28] *Id.* at 19.

[29] FIXING BAGRAM, *supra* note 7, at 7; *See Maqaleh v. Gates*, 605 F.3d 84 (D.C. Cir. 2010).

[30] *See Bowman et al.*, *supra* note 10.

31 Bovarnick *supra* note 27, at 9 n.1. It is notable that when the new $60 million facility was opened, U.S. authorities said that it had the capacity to hold 1100 detainees. It now holds nearly 1700.

32 See Alissa J. Rubin, *Afghans Detail Detention in 'Black Jail' at U.S. Base*, N.Y. Times, Nov. 28, 2009; Joshua Partlow & Julie Tate, *2 Afghans Allege Abuse at U.S. site*, Wash. Post, Nov. 28, 2009; Hillary Anderson, *Red Cross Confirms 'Second Jail' at Bagram, Afghanistan*, BBC News, May 11, 2010. *See also* REG'L POLICY INITIATIVE ON AFG. AND PAK., OPEN SOC'Y FOUND., CONFINEMENT CONDITIONS IN A U.S. SCREENING FACILITY AT THE BAGRAM AIR BASE 2 (2010) [hereinafter CONFINEMENT CONDITIONS] .

33 It is unclear whether the ICRC has access to these detainees, and even if it does, its assessments of their treatment and the facility's conditions are not public.

34 *See generally* CONFINEMENT CONDITIONS, supra note 32.

35 Kimberly Dozier, *AP Exclusive: Terror Suspects Held Weeks in Secret*, ASSOCIATED PRESS, Apr. 8, 2011.

36 U.S. DEP'T OF THE ARMY, HUMAN INTELLIGENCE COLLECTOR OPERATIONS, FM 2-22.3, 2006.

37 See HUMAN RIGHTS FIRST, THE U.S. ARMY FIELD MANUAL ON INTERROGATION: A STRONG DOCUMENT IN NEED OF REVISION (2010), *available at* http://www.humanrightsfirst.org/our-work/law-and-security/torture-and-accountability/appendix-m-of-the-army-field-manual/further-reading/; *see also* Letter from 14 Former Interrogators and Intelligence Officials to Robert Gates, Def. Sec (Nov. 15, 2010) *available at* http://www.humanrightsfirst.org/our-work/law-and-security/torture-and-accountability/appendix-m-of-the-army-field-manual/letter-from-interrogators-and-intelligence-officials/.

38 Eric Schmitt, *U.S. Shifts, Giving Detainee Names to the Red Cross*, N.Y. Times, Aug. 22, 2009.

39 The Detainee Review Board Procedures at Bagram Theater Internment Facility (BTIF) Afghanistan issued July 2009, attached as an appendix to Brief of Respondent-Appellants appeal to the U.S. Court of Appeals for the District of Columbia, *Maqaleh v. Gates*, Nos. 09-5265, 09-5266, 09-5277 (D.C. Cir. Sept. 14, 2009), indicates that the BTIF commander must assess whether the detainee meets criteria for transfer to the BTIF "normally within 14 days of the detainee's capture." This statement is absent from the superseding July 2010 memo that represents current policy. *See* MEMORANDUM, *supra* note 4. Based on our interviews with former detainees, prisoners continue to be segregated in separate facilities prior to their transfer to the BTIF, in some cases for longer than 14 days.

40 Human Rights First interviews with former detainees in Kabul, Afghanistan, 2010, 2011 (on file with author); *see also* CONFINEMENT CONDITIONS *supra* note 32, at 8.

41 MEMORANDUM, *supra* note 4, at 4 (Significantly, President Obama in his Executive Order of Mar. 7, 2011 creating a new review process for detainees at Guantanamo Bay similarly provides detainees there with "personal representatives.").

42 MEMORANDUM, *supra* note 4 at 3.

43 *Id.* at 6.

44 *Id.* at 5.

45 According to the July 2010 memorandum, those legally detained must be either:

a. Persons who planned, authorized, committed, or aided the terrorist attacks that occurred on September 11, 2001, and persons who harbored those responsible for those attacks;

b. Persons who were part of, or substantially supported, Taliban or al-Qaida forces or associated forces that are engaged in hostilities against the United States or its coalition partners, including any person who has committed a belligerent act, or has directly supported hostilities, in aid of such enemy armed forces.

See id. at 2.

46 *Id.* at 11.

47 The ACLU had not yet completed its review of these documents by the time of the publication of this report.

48 Interview with William Lietzau, *supra* note 11, stating that "about a dozen" third-country nationals are in this situation.

49 Interview with Hans Klemm, U.S. Rule of Law Ambassador, in Kabul, Afg. (Feb. 8, 2011).

50 Pejic, *supra* note 6, at 388.

51 Brief of Amici Curiae in support of the Petitioners at 5, Rahman v. Gates, No. 10-320 (D.C. Dist. Mar. 28, 2011) (citing HJC 3239/02 Marab v. IDF Commander in the West Bank IsrSC 57(2) 349, ¶ 1 [2003]).

52 For a description of the course, *see* Bovarnick, *supra* note 27, Appendix B.

53 This is the traditional dress in Afghanistan, consisting of a tunic-length shirt and loose-fitting pants.

54 Many Afghans have only one name, rather than a first and last name.

55 Human Rights First was brought into the hearing after the detainee stated his name for the record, and JTF 435 did not respond to a request for his name before the release of this report. JTF 435 also refused to provide any information about the outcomes of any of the DRB hearings we observed. Human Rights First has filed a Freedom of Information Act request seeking that information.

56 Ray Rivera, *In an Afghan Village, Living in Fear of Both Sides*, N.Y.Times, April 23, 2011.

57 *See* Open Soc'y Inst. & The Liaison Office, Strangers at the Door: Night Raids by International Forces Lose Hearts and Minds of Afghans (2010) [hereinafter Night Raids]; Human Rights, U.N.Assistance Mission in Afg. & Afg. Indep. Human Rights Comm'n, Afghanistan Annual Report 2010 on Protection of Civilians in Armed Conflict 36, 51 (2011).

58 Meeting with Vice Admiral Harward, Commander of Combined Joint Interagency Task Force (CJIATF) 435, in Kabul, Afg., Feb. 2010, reporting that most detainees at the DFIP are held "less than a year." In 2010 alone, however, JTF 435 statistics indicate that 1364 detainees entered the DFIP, while only 597 were released. *See* Joint Taskforce 435 Detention and Release Statistics (on file with author).

59 *See, e.g.*, Hamid Shalizi, *NATO Air Strike Killed Two Afghan Children in East: Officials*, Yahoo News, Mar. 15, 2011; Alissa Rubin & Sangar Rahimi, *Nine Afghan Boys Collecting Firewood Killed by NATO Helicopter*s, N.Y. Times, Mar. 2, 2011; Alissa Rubin, *Afghan Team Says NATO Killed Civilians in Strikes*, N.Y. Times, Feb. 27, 2011.

60 *See* Night Raids, *supra* note 57, at 4 (concluding that "Afghans remain critical of the behavior and lack of accountability of Afghan and international forces who engage in night raids, as well as their subsequent detention procedures. These concerns reinforce negative perceptions about international forces, eroding much of the strategic value of other positive policy changes related to civilian casualties and detention.").

61 *See* Poll *supra* note 8, at 31.

62 Pejic, *supra* note 6, at 382-83.

63 *Id.* at 387 (stating that "If a person is kept in internment/administrative detention despite a final release order, that is a clear case of arbitrary detention.").

64 The Constitution of Afghanistan, Jan. 3, 2004, art. 51.

65 ICCPR *supra* note 5, art. 9.5.

66 United States Army Combined Arms Center, Commander's Emergency Response Program, Handbook 09-27, Chapter 4, *available at* http://usacac.army.mil/cac2/call/docs/09-27/ch-4.asp.

67 *See* COMISAF Assessment, *supra* note 1; *see also* Night Raids, *supra* note 57 (finding similar problems and making similar recommendations).

68 See Chris Rogers, Campaign for Innocent Victims in Conflict, Addressing Civilian Harm in Afghanistan, Policies and Practices of International Forces (2010).

69 Declaration of William K. Lietzau at 1, *Maqaleh v. Rumsfeld*, 605 F.3d 84 (D.C. Cir. 2010) (No. 08-2143).

70 Farah Stockman, *Kinder Prison, Swifter Justice for U.S. Detainees in Afghanistan*, Boston Globe, Jan. 18, 2011 ("Not everyone is eligible for the rehabilitation programs or speedy release; 119 inmates have been detained for more than two years, about 80 of whom Harward said the United States intends to keep indefinitely because they are third-country nationals or Al Qaeda affiliates deemed a serious security threat outside Afghanistan.").

71 Int'l Crisis Grp., Reforming Afghanistan's Broken Judiciary (2010).

72 Liana Sun Wyler & Kenneth Katzman, Cong. Research Serv., Afghanistan: U.S. Rule of Law and Justice Sector Assistance (2010).

73 Human Rights, U.N. Assistance Mission in Afg., Arbitrary Detention in Afghanistan: A Call for Action (2009).

74 U.S. Dep't of State, *2010 Human Rights Report: Afghanistan*, Country Rep. on Hum. Rts. Prac., *available at* http://www.state.gov/g/drl/rls/hrrpt/2010/sca/154477.htm.

75 U.S. Dep't. of State, Office of Inspector Gen., Rule of Law Programs in Afghanistan, ISP-I-08-09 (2008).

76 *Boumediene v. Bush*, 553 U.S. 723, 798 (2008).